... this is Africa ...

... and this is my country. Nigeria.

This is the city of Enugu. I was born there.

When I was a boy in Africa, we did not have much. It was hard.

But we were kids and we played football all the time.

We had no football pitches, or goals, or kit. All the kids played in the street.

Nobody had shoes, or football boots. And we had rocks for goalposts. But it didn't matter, we just wanted to play.

I was good at football, so when I was 15 I got to play for the team Arab Contractors. This was in Cairo, in Egypt.

This was a big change for me. I had to be on my own in a very different country.

And now I play for Portsmouth in the English Premier League.

And I play for my country, too –
Nigeria. At Portsmouth I play with
Kanu, who is also from Nigeria.

When Portsmouth won the F.A. Cup in 2008, Kanu scored the winning goal. It was so fantastic - for me, for Pompey and for Nigeria!

I am a striker. I like getting goals.

And now I do it for a job, with one of the best clubs in England. That's not bad, after starting so long ago and so far away!

At school in Africa I used to read lots of Charles Dickens. Now I think Shakespeare and Dickens are the best. I just think reading is cool.

Books help you understand about life. The biggest thing I ever did was to learn to read.

That's much more important than football. Trust me!

Plays are cool, too. And acting. This is me in the theatre. **Hamlet** and **Macbeth** are fantastic plays. Maybe one day I will act on the stage.

'Is that a ball I see before me?'

13

My career so far has been great. But I had to work hard. Winning the F.A. Cup with Portsmouth has been the best thing so far. Now I just want to win more cups and get better as a player.

That's not a lot to ask, is it?